Contents

You can find words shown in bold, **like this** in the Glossary.

What is glass?

Glass is a material that people make in **factories**. It is not a **natural** material. These thin sheets of glass have just been made. They will be put into window frames.

Glass is an important material. It is waterproof and you can see through it. We make many different things from glass. All the things on this page are made from glass.

Breaking glass

Glass objects break into pieces if they are dropped or if they are hit. The broken pieces have very sharp edges. Because glass breaks like this, we say that it is **brittle**.

Glass for doors and windows is made strong to stop it shattering into sharp pieces. This special glass is called safety glass. It may shatter into tiny round pieces, or it may crack without shattering.

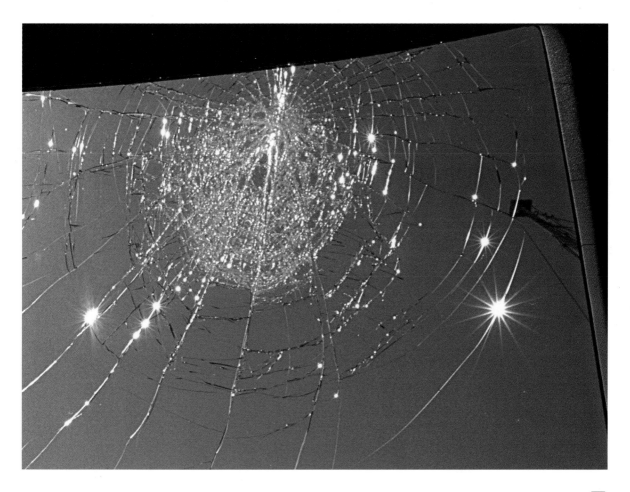

See-through glass

All glass lets light through. Some glass
is **transparent**. You can see straight
through transparent glass. Some glass
is coloured with **chemicals**. Some
glass is clear.

Some glass is **opaque**. It lets light through but you cannot see straight through it. Bathroom windows often have opaque glass so that nobody can see in.

Heat and chemicals

Glass does not burn when it is heated up. Fire fighters wear fabrics made with thin **fibres** of glass to protect themselves from flames. Glass does go runny when it gets very hot, though.

Scientists store **chemicals** in glass bottles and tubes. This is because glass is not damaged by most chemicals. Strong chemicals would eat away metal or plastic containers.

Making glass

Glass is mostly made from sand, just
like the sand on a beach. The sand is
mixed with other **chemicals**. Then it
is heated until it **melts** to make a
thick liquid.

When the hot liquid cools down, it sets to make glass. To make thin sheets of glass, the liquid is spread onto the top of a huge pool of very hot, runny metal.

Shaping glass

Some glass objects are made in **moulds**.
Hot, liquid glass is poured into a mould.
When the glass has cooled, the mould is
opened and the object is taken out.

Some objects are made by glass blowing.
A glass blower puts a blob of hot, liquid
glass on the end of a tube. He blows
along the tube and the glass blows up
like a balloon, then sets.

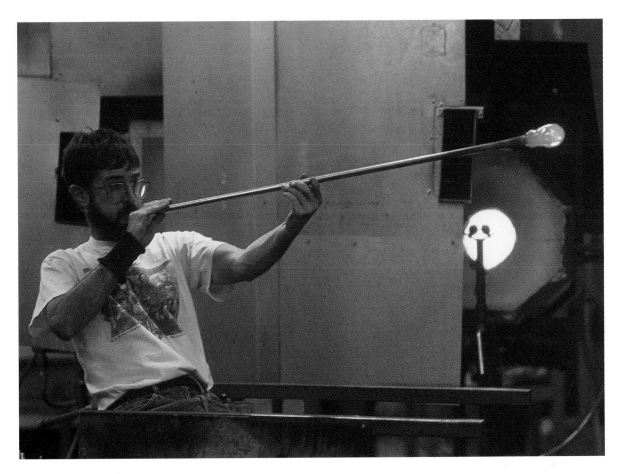

Making patterns

You can decorate glass by making patterns on its surface. This artist is making patterns on a glass bottle by cutting into them with a **cutting disc**.

You can also make patterns by **etching**. Patterns are painted onto the glass with special **chemicals** that eat away at the surface. A pattern is left when the chemicals are wiped off.

Mirrors and lenses

A mirror is made of a sheet of glass.
The smooth back surface of the glass
is painted with silvery paint. Light that
goes into the mirror bounces off the
paint and out again.

A magnifying glass has a piece of glass in it called a lens. The lens is thicker in the middle than at the edges. It bends light to make things look bigger than they really are.

Glass in buildings

Glass used in windows is called glazing. Windows let light from the sun into buildings. They also stop heat escaping from warm buildings and keep the wind and rain out.

In cold countries, many buildings have double glazing to keep the insides of the buildings warm. Each window has two sheets of glass, with a small gap between the sheets.

Decorating with glass

Glass often looks pretty when light bounces off it, or goes through it. Some **jewellers** use glass instead of expensive gemstones such as diamonds to make jewellery and ornaments.

Small pieces of coloured glass are used to make patterns. These **stained glass** windows look beautiful when sunlight from outside floods through them.

High-tech glass

This **communications cable** has long, thin glass **fibres** inside. They are called optical fibres. Flashes of light travel along the fibres, carrying telephone calls.

This boat is being made from a very strong material called glass-reinforced plastic. The material is made of glass and plastic. It is a stronger material than glass or plastic on their own.

Recycling glass

Glass bottles, jars and other glass objects can be used again to make new glass things. This is called recycling. Sometimes there are bins for glass of different colours at collection centres.

The glass is taken to a glass-making **factory**. It is sorted into different colours and smashed into pieces. Then it is **melted** and made into new objects.

Fact file

Glass is made in **factories**. It is not a **natural** material.

Plain glass is **brittle**. It smashes into pieces easily. Safety glass is much stronger than plain glass.

Glass lets light through. It can be plain or coloured.

Glass does not burn. It goes soft and runny when it gets very hot.

Glass is waterproof. It does not rot away when it is wet.

Electricity does not flow through glass.

Heat does flow through glass, but not very well.

Glass is not attracted by **magnets**.

Would you believe it?

Some of the biggest glass objects in the world are mirrors in huge telescopes. Scientists use telescopes to look into space. The biggest telescope mirror is six metres across. That is as wide as three grown-ups lying end to end!

Glossary

brittle   a brittle material snaps when it is bent or stretched

chemicals   special materials that are used in factories and homes to do many jobs, including cleaning and protecting.

communications cable   cable that carries telephone calls, fax messages and e-mail

cutting disc   tool for cutting glass. It has a circle of metal with a sharp edge. As the disc spins, the edge cuts into the glass.

electricity   form of energy. We use electricity to make electric machines work.

etching   making a pattern on the surface of a material by letting chemicals eat away at the surface

factory   place where things are made using machines

fibre   thin thread of material. Glass fibres are threads of glass as thin as a hair.

jeweller   person who makes jewellery

magnet   object that attracts iron and steel

melt   turn from solid to liquid

mould   block of material that is hollowed out in the shape of an object

natural   comes from plants, animals or rocks in the earth

opaque   lets light through but is not see-through

stained glass   glass that has been coloured by chemicals

transparent   see-through

More books to read

What is See-Through?
Nina Morgan
Heinemann Library, 1996

My World of Science: Light and Dark
Angela Royston
Heinemann Library, 2001

Images: Materials and Their Properties
Big Book Compilation
Heinemann Library, 1999

Science All Around Me: Materials
Karen Bryant-Mole
Heinemann Library, 1996

Find Out About Glass
Henry Pluckrose,
Franklin Watts

I Can Help Recycle Rubbish
Franklin Watts

Index